# A GUIDE
to
# MIDDLE SCHOOL
and
# BEYOND

By

Mike Turnbull

A Guide to Middle School and Beyond
Copyright © 2016 by Mike Turnbull
Rivershore Books
Cover design by Rivershore Books
Cover photo by Mike Turnbull
Photos by Mike Turnbull unless otherwise noted
Author photo courtesy of author

ISBN-13: 978-0692696330
ISBN-10: 0692696334
First published in 2016

PRINTED IN THE UNITED STATES OF AMERICA

# PREFACE

I want you to know that I attended Junior High School in 1971–1973. I took seventh and part of eighth grade at Chipman Junior High in Alameda, California, and the rest of eighth grade at a school I can't remember the name of in Browns Mills, New Jersey. My dad, who was in the U.S. Navy, was transferred from Alameda Naval Air Station to the Lakehurst Naval Air Station in New Jersey early in my eighth-grade year.

I also taught 7th and 8th grade social studies classes from 1981 to 1993. My teaching jobs were all in Minnesota; Lake Park, Ely, Norwood-Young America and Wadena. I have taught and coached at the college level since 1993 and continue to do so today.

I have always wanted to do some writing about this time in the lives of young people. I was ready to attempt this several years ago when a book called *The Diary of a Wimpy Kid* hit the market. It seemed kind of pointless to attempt to put my thoughts on the subject to paper.

Please understand that I in no way claim to be any kind of an expert on the subject of adolescence or the middle school education system, but I do feel I have a few ideas worth sharing.

This is neither a success guide nor a survival guide, merely a guide. Thoughts and ideas I hope you will mull over and give consideration to. If you find anything that helps, that's great!

Mike Turnbull

# DEDICATION

To all my student-athletes that I have taught and coached over the past thirty-five years: You are all and have always been the reason I get up every morning and happily head off to school. I have been blessed to have had the opportunity to be in the education field all this time. You have all provided many insightful moments and fond memories.

I hope all of you are well and thriving.

Photo by Mike Flaten

# SPECIAL THANK YOU

Thanks to my sister, Lisa Rahja, an elementary teacher, and my nephew, Grant Rahja, a freshman at UW-Madison. Your input during the writing of this book was invaluable to me.

# TABLE OF CONTENTS

"The function of education is to teach one to think intensively and to think critically. Intelligence plus character — that is the goal of true education."
-Dr. Martin Luther King, Jr.

# CHAPTER ONE
## The Year Before

Let us assume you are in sixth grade and will be transitioning to middle school next year. Next year you will be moving into the next phase of the educational process. Many of you may be making the move to middle school in your 6th grade year. Either way, we are talking about your last year of elementary school.

First of all, enjoy this year, because it is the last time you will be at the top of the student pecking order for the next two or three years. Seventh graders will assume the bottom rung of the ladder, with eighth and possibly ninth graders above you. If you are in a smaller setting and making the move to the high school, you won't be back on top again until your senior year.

This would be a good time to start understanding the concept of *networking*. What I mean is, start making a list of the people you know who are already at the middle school and especially those who will be there when you get there. Think: friends, siblings, neighbors, teachers, coaches, councilors, staff members, principals, etc. You will want these people to know who you are; they are all people who will be able to make the transition easier and help you succeed along the way.

If you have older brothers and sisters who have attended the school before you, be sure to work on carving your own unique identity right away. You have to understand if they have left the performance bar set high or low for you. I can tell you, as an ex-secondary teacher, when you get a kid in your class or on your team that is the younger brother or sister of someone you have taught or coached before, it is hard for a while to separate the two in your head. Don't be surprised if a teacher or coach actually uses your older brother or sister's name when referring to you. It will probably take a little time, but keep working on establishing your identity. It might be scary to think of this, but it is possible—especially in small towns—that your mom and dad may have attended that school also and had the same teachers. You do the research.

You will probably have the opportunity to register for classes and attend some kind of orientation session sometime this year in preparation for next year. Do not take this lightly; it is very important that you fit your course selection to your educational needs and desires. I say "needs" because there will be courses that are necessary and required for you to take. I say "desires" because you will be able to take a few classes because they interest you and you choose to take those classes. These classes are called electives.

If you have any thoughts of going to college eventually, start laying the groundwork now. Try to take challenging classes, and if a foreign language is offered, take it. You might have to do some testing to determine what level of English and Math classes you are allowed to take. Take the highest levels of the classes offered if you think you will eventually be going to college. It is okay if you decide not to go to college and decide to seek a career through a vocational school, if your interests lie in mechanical, plumbing, computers, welding, carpentry, etc. Follow your passion; it will eventually lead you to a career. Whatever you start to lean a little toward, research it and still consider the right classes to help you explore your options. I knew early on I didn't want to be stuck in an office; I wanted to stay around athletics and I enjoyed working with kids. That eventually led me to teaching and coaching.

You might be thinking about now, "What is this guy talking about? I am going into 7th grade and he is talking college?" Don't be alarmed; you are trying to prepare for a successful future, don't be afraid to project ahead. The things you do now and over the next couple of years to continue your educational journey will prove to be invaluable to you in high school and beyond. If you are not willing to get serious about your education, start practicing this phrase, "Do you want fries with that?" You will need to know this for the job you will be doing in the future.

If you are moving into a new school for your seventh-grade year, take the time to go tour around the school and familiarize yourself with the building, the grounds, and the athletic facilities. Whenever you get your class schedule, take it to the school, walk the halls, and find all your classrooms, locker, the cafeteria, the bathrooms, the administration office, teachers' lounge, gym, auditorium, or any other places you expect to frequent throughout the school year. The better you know your physical environment, the more comfortable you will feel when you get there. When you are visiting the school, don't be afraid to introduce yourself to people and ask any questions you might have.

Watch the mail, the local newspaper, and the school's website for any announcements about sign-ups for sports, clubs, or activities at the school that you might be interested in joining. Stay on top of this information, because some activities, fall sports for example, might start before the first day of classes and you don't want to miss out on something that you want to try out for or participate in.

*The doors to success*

*Not where you want to spent a lot of your time*

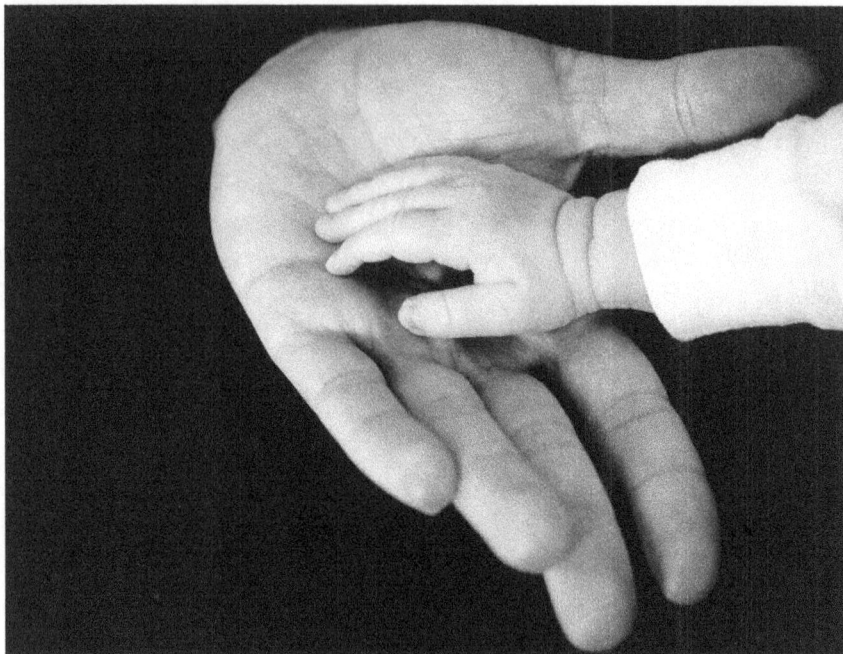

*Young or old, we all need a helping hand.*
(Photo by Leanne Metzler on Stock Snap)

*Dream Big!*

# CHAPTER TWO
## First Day of School

This is always an exciting day. Remember, it is all about attitude! You are the only one who can determine the attitude and approach that you are going to take to any given day. Other people do not dictate to you if you are going to be in a good mood or a bad mood; it is up to you and you alone.

You have been in elementary school for several years now, but today is different; it is the first day of Middle School. As soon as you get to school, find your friends and get together. Catch up with the ones you didn't see over the summer. Next, seek new faces, kids new to town or from elementary schools other than your own. Also, don't be afraid to seek out the kids who seem lonely or afraid, welcome them in, and expand your face-to-face social network. For all you know, you might meet your next best friend. Don't be surprised if some of your classmates look a little different than what you remember from last spring; you probably do, too. It has been close to three months since you may have seen some of them. You are all at an age where you might be going through some physical changes (puberty). Things happen, your voice changes, hair grows in places you didn't have it before, and some kids have growth spurts and some may have entered into the wonderful world of zits and menstrual cycles. Just take it all in; you and your classmates are all maturing and at different rates. You will find you are the same as others in some cases and a little ahead of or behind with other things. No matter where you fall on the physical maturity scale, don't be alarmed if you are behind and don't get cocky if you are ahead. We all seem to get to a level of sameness at some point in time.

If you are a boy, don't be surprised if seventh-grade girls are not showing much interest in you. You are about to find out that they tend to be more interested in the older boys in school. They might be comparing you to eighth- and ninth-grade boys and, let's face it, in their eyes, you just don't match up. If you want to impress them, just chill out for a while and play it cool. Acting stupid is not going to impress them, punching them in the arm won't help your cause either, and roughhousing with your friends in front of those girls doesn't make you look any more mature. Try being polite, offer your assistance when it can be offered, and open a door for them every once in a while. Drop a sincere compliment here and there and be respectful. Dress like you actually care what you look like; smelling good doesn't hurt, either.

Girls, don't be too hard on your male classmates. You are probably right; for the most part, they are not very mature. For some reason, God has designed it so that girls tend to mature ahead of boys. So, be patient; most of them will catch up sometime. Just keep an eye on them and don't be afraid to offer a little guidance. I know the older boys seem to be a little more attractive at this point in time, but be careful; they have had a year or two working on how to impress younger girls and they may not always be showing their true selves.

If nothing else, learn to take care of each other and watch each other's backs; you are all in this new environment together. Everyone is trying to find their own way, their own identity, and what their niche is. Everyone is going to make mistakes and have successes, individually and in group situations. It is okay to admit when you feel scared, confused, or stressed out. Don't forget what I said about having each other's backs. The concept is social support. Every student should feel safe, comfortable, and welcomed at school. Bullying kids less fortunate or popular as yourself, or being bullied by kids, is never acceptable. You will find yourself on both ends of the scale at various times in your life. Stay true to who you are and don't be afraid to exert your will. It is better to be a leader than a follower. The followers only ever see the back of the person in front of them; leaders get to see all the world has to offer firsthand. It is difficult at times to step away from what the "in crowd" is doing. If you witness bullying or are being bullied yourself, don't fear standing up and doing or saying something about it. Any school employee should be able to help you. Bullying is easy; being compassionate is hard. As human beings, besides air, water, and food, we also deserve and need to be wanted and know that someone cares about us. You will find that people gravitate to you when they realize you truly care about them. Find classmates you are comfortable sharing your various emotions with, along with your daily issues or problems. You might find it refreshing to find out other kids are thinking about these types of things also. If things are going well for you, keep your eye out for kids who are struggling and offer your support.

It might only be the first day, but try to keep in mind things will be all right in the end and if it is not all right it must not be the end. One last heads' up: don't be surprised if you have a bunch of homework by the end of the day. It is an old teaching theory that is still widely used by teachers today. The theory is for the teacher to start out tough and demanding right from the start and loosen up as the year progresses. Just roll with it; everything gets better as you become more comfortable with the system.

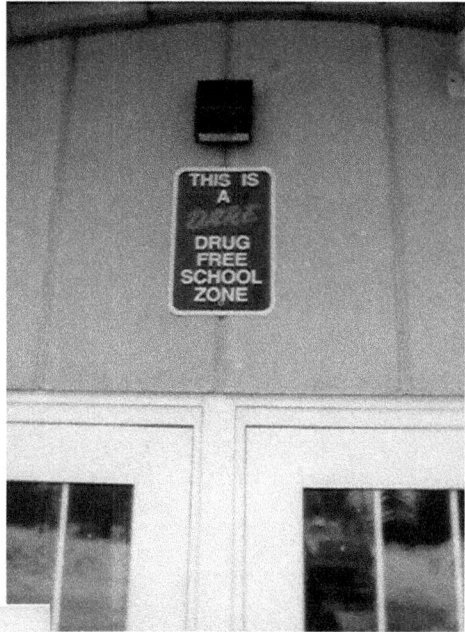

*Know and follow the rules.*

*We always have a choice!*

Mike Turnbull

*Your call!*

*Just be you!*
(Photo by Dimitry Rutashny on Unsplash)

# CHAPTER THREE
## You Made It

Let us assume for all practical purposes you survived the first day of middle school, it went well, and you have high hopes for the future. I hope you had someone at home you could share the events of the first day with. Parents love the question, "So how did it go?"

When you get a general question like this from your parents, offer an answer right away. This allows you to continue to control the conversation (inquiry). If you don't offer an answer or just come back with something like, "it was okay," "fine," or the ultimate killer, "whatever," your parents will follow up with a barrage of questions such as, "Did you like your teachers?" "How was lunch?" "Do you like your classes?" or "Did you meet any new kids?" Don't let this frustrate you; if you have parents or someone else in your life showing this kind of interest in you, smile; you are blessed. A lot of kids don't have these types of people in their lives. It is good to be loved!

If you are a child who does not have caring parents for whatever reason (death, divorce, separations, abandonment, drug abuse, alcoholism, imprisonment, etc.), seek guidance. Teachers, counselors, coaches, advisers, grandparents, or older siblings; find someone you can openly go to and let them into your life. Some of these people may present themselves or you might have to seek them out on your own. Either way, find someone. Everyone needs a mentor. I was lucky enough to have great parents, but I also had very productive relationships with many of my coaches over the years.

You probably have homework, so get to it right away. Find a quiet place where you are comfortable. Eliminate distractions, and shut your phone off! You don't need to be distracted by text messages, tweets, or any other incoming messages or social media. Better yet, shut your phone off and put it in another room, so you are not tempted to set your homework aside and check out your phone. If there is a television in the room, unplug it. That should do it . . . oh, yeah; take the headphones off. Despite anything you have heard or read, there is really no music to listen to that will have a positive impact on studying or retention of information. I promise, your phone, television, and music downloads will still be there when you are done with your homework. It will probably also give you an ego boost when you find out how many people tried to contact you while you were finishing your homework. How great will it be when you can announce to all your followers, "I am done with my homework!"

If you have to use a computer to complete your assigned work, it will be up to you to be disciplined enough to not surf the internet or tap into social media outlets. It is called delayed gratification. Try not to reward yourself until you have accomplished something.

Years ago I remember watching a video, which was produced by a high school coach in Massachusetts. I am sorry but I can't remember what his name was or where he coached. I do remember that some of what he said had a huge impact on my thinking and how I tried to go about my life. Basically, his message was: if you want to succeed, work when others play, study when others sleep, and practice and sleep when others party!

My dad always said nothing good happens after midnight. I didn't know what he was talking about when I was in junior high, and I didn't really have any opportunities to challenge his theory. I will admit that when I was in high school, he was right. I broke a few midnight curfews and I can tell you, nothing good ever came from it. In college and especially in graduate school, I had to pull a few all-nighters studying for a test or writing a paper. Those all-night study sessions may have served their purpose, but despite the sense of accomplishment, the next day at school was brutal. To be honest, if I hadn't waited until the last final night to study or complete the assignment, the all-nighters wouldn't have been necessary.

Bob Montibello, my college baseball coach, always said if you are ever wondering if you are doing the right thing or something good, ask yourself if you could call your mom right at that exact moment and say, "Mom, guess what I am doing right now!" Coach said if you can't make that phone call, you probably shouldn't be doing what you are doing.

Last year, one of my ex-players called me to tell me about a job interview she had with a biomedical engineering company. At the end of the interview process, she was one of four finalists, from a pool of hundreds of candidates, for two jobs the company was offering. To complete the next phase of the hiring process, she was asked to take a drug test and turn over all her social media accounts on the spot. She agreed to do this because she was confident she had nothing to hide. Her drug test came up clean and the company found nothing in her social media accounts that caused any alarm, so she was offered one of the jobs. As for the other three finalists, two refused to take the drug test or turn over their social media accounts and one was eliminated because of incriminatory pictures found in his/her social media accounts. I realize this may not seem significant to most seventh graders—you are not worried about getting jobs with biomedical companies—but you need to realize what you put into your body and what you put on the internet can impact your life, health, and the view that other people have of you. It may take years to build a positive reputation, but it only takes a minute to destroy a positive reputation.

Let's get back on topic. We were talking about homework. Hopefully, you are not sitting at home wondering if you had homework. If you are, call or text a classmate and find out. If you do have homework, hopefully you brought the right books and notes home with you. Now, let's back up to earlier today at school. At the end of class, did the teacher announce a homework assignment? If they did, did you write down what the assignment was and when it was due? Does the assignment have to be turned in or were you just asked to do some reading to prepare for the next time the class meets? Do you have to be ready to present in class or possibly take a test or quiz? The next question is, did you bring home the things you need to complete the homework? If you have done all of this, pat yourself on the back and get to work. If you haven't done the things necessary to complete an assignment, kick yourself in the butt, and either start thinking up a great excuse or plan a way to get to school early tomorrow and maybe you'll have time to complete the assignment. If you have a test or a quiz, good luck! (Sarcasm Alert)

Now, let's review. Did the teacher announce the assignment at the end of class? Ask yourself, "Was I listening?" Or were you busy packing your book bag or talking to a friend? The teacher probably announced the assignment; did you write it down or did you leave it up to chance that you would remember? You have way too much going on in your life. Write it down! Get all the details, what the assignment is, when it is due, how it will be used, and—for a little more motivation—how many points it is worth and how it will impact your grade. When you are standing at your locker at the end of the day, do a mental and physical review and figure out what you need to bring home. If you are not sure, bring all your books, your iPad, and notebooks home with you. You won't get caught off guard when you get home, and as an additional bonus it creates the image that you are serious about your academics.

When it comes down to creating excuses for not having a homework assignment done, forget it! Your teacher has probably heard them all. Even if you have a teacher in their first year of teaching, keep in mind that they were once a student and they still have

11

heard or used the excuses themselves.

You don't have your homework done. As far as getting to school early the next day is concerned, you are probably out of luck. You can't drive, you can't change the bus schedule, and most likely you probably won't wake up early enough to walk to school early.

If you have a test or a quiz the next day and you are not prepared, you should probably just try to figure out how you are going to cover for those points later. You might also consider the moral dilemma of cheating on the exam. Be careful; choosing to cheat is a slippery slope. If you get caught, you will most likely receive a zero on the exam and your teacher will assume you are dishonest and need to be watched in the future. Detention might also be in your immediate future. If you are not caught, you will consider the same action later on. You now are in a situation where you do not really know or understand the information and you will not retain it as a base for building future knowledge. You may have not been caught, but you will experience paranoia and guilt. Even though your teacher is unaware of the fact that you cheated, your peers know and you have created the image of "cheater" in their minds. (Reputation?)

If college is in your future plans (I hope it is, but if not that is okay, too), consider this: if you are caught cheating or plagiarizing in a college course, that is grounds for being kicked out of class and receiving an "F" for the semester. If it is a serious or repeated offense, you can be kicked out of school. Just remember an education is a privilege, not a right. By all means, try to stay off the slippery slope; it is your personal responsibility to prepare for class. As you get older and move along in your academic career, there are fewer and fewer people babysitting you through the process. Eventually, the ultimate burden to succeed is on you.

*Webster's Dictionary defines "Excuse" as 1. To make apology for: try to remove blame from; 2. To accept an excuse for; 3. To free or let off from doing something; 4. To serve as an acceptable reason or explanation for something said or done.* The bottom line is, a teacher cannot grade an excuse, so there are no grade points awarded for an excuse.

*On the other hand, Webster's Dictionary defines the word "Execute" as 1. To put into effect: carry out: PERFORM; 2. To do what is provided or required by.* A teacher can work with this.

It comes down to habits; they can be good and produce positive results or they can be bad and produce negative consequences. You just have to ask yourself, "What are my goals and what am I trying to accomplish?" Then ask yourself, "Am I doing the things necessary to attain those goals and accomplishments?"

I have taught and coached for 35 years now. Over the years, I have come to divide students and athletes into two categories, "Players" and "Pretenders." "Players" tend to get things done and not spend a lot of time talking about it. "Pretenders" tend to spend a lot of time talking about it but rarely seem to produce.

I have heard people say, "Don't judge me." I am here to tell you people will judge you. They will form opinions about you and what you do. You can't control what people think or say about you, but you do have the power to influence it. Just remember, people hear what you say (audio) and they see what you do (visual). You build a reputation from what you do, not necessarily from what you say. You can say, "I think it is important to study and get good grades" (audio). But you can forget to turn in homework assignments, not listen in class or take notes, or watch television when you should have been studying (visual). The trick is to get audio and visual to match up. You are judged on visual. Your reputation can be enhanced by what you say, but your actions are the proof.

The first day of school, you were probably too nervous and rushed to pay a lot of attention to the ways information was presented to you around school. I am talking about announcements, schedules, meetings, available activities, clubs, and organizations. It all comes at you in many ways, so if you want to stay informed, pay attention.

First of all, if your school has a website, which it most likely does, try to visit it on a regular basis. Check it at night, in the morning, and once during the day if the opportunity presents itself. There might also be a school newsletter or paper; find out how to obtain one and how often it comes out.

Find the bulletin boards around campus and check those out. When you are walking the halls, keep your head up and read signs and posters on the walls. If your school has television monitors in the halls or common areas check those out. There might also be a digital sign somewhere in your school parking lot that streams school information; take the time to read it. Some schools still do homerooms and morning announcements; listen to them!

You don't want to miss an opportunity to attend an event, join a club or organization, go to a dance, take a trip, or — worse yet — eat free food! Just pay attention to what is going on.

Try to get involved in activities at school. Everyone should; it makes the school experience that much more fun and rewarding. You feel a lot more connected to the school and your classmates. If you are looking for things to do or join and you haven't heard anything, ask around. Ask an 8th grader, teacher, counselor, office secretary, or coach. Most likely, if any of these people don't know, they can probably direct you to someone who does. Don't let a little shyness or apprehension keep you from getting the information you are seeking. If you wait too long, you may miss something altogether or it might be too late to join.

*You made it!*
(Photo by Danielle Macinnes from Stock Snap)

*Capture the moments . . .*
(Photo by Tom Sodoge from Stock Snap)

*Time is passing; are you?*
(Photo by freestock.org from Stock Snap)

*Step away from the video games and get
outside for a little while.*

# CHAPTER FOUR
## Moving Forward

Now, is the time to start thinking about college. I'm serious; you need a plan. You are now a year away from entering high school. You are already at a point where the decisions you make can have a definite impact on your future.

I'm not trying to scare you. I just want you to be alerted to the fact that you are now laying the groundwork for your future. Some families and parents that were thinking ahead started this process in preschool. Some people believe that where you attend preschool, kindergarten, and elementary school will determine what secondary and post-secondary schools you get into later, which will ultimately affect your career choices in the future.

I don't necessarily refute this, but I have spent my whole life in the public school system and I am a proponent. With this said, please understand, the majority of this book is aimed at students making their way through public and state school systems.

If college is in your future, commit to a plan. Take the most challenging classes available: upper math, sciences, and a foreign language. If electives are available, choose something you enjoy but that is still challenging. If at some time you decide college is not what you are destined for, you will still need a plan. For example, if you want to be a plumber (great occupation; I pay my plumber a lot of money because I can't do plumbing), you still need a plan. Math is required, social skills are important, and business sense comes in handy. If you really don't have a clue about your future, don't be scared; you are in the majority. Expand your education and you will find your niche.

Join as many clubs, activities, organizations, and sports as you can handle. If you have the gifts to do so, look into band, choir, or speech. Also do as much volunteer work as you can. You are building a resume for the future. The more liberal your education, the more exposure you will get to new ideas and career options.

Don't bank on sports to be your ticket to college. Of all the kids that participate in sports, very few parlay that into a college scholarship and even fewer to a professional contract.

Out of all the kids I have coached or taught over the past 35 years, only 4 have made professional money and a little over a dozen have received athletic scholarships to colleges. Thousands have received academic scholarships and moved on to successful careers. I have coached some very talented student-athletes, but the vast majority of those that have experienced success in their futures beyond that point have done so on factors other than athletics.

I coach at a two-year college and when recruiters from four-year schools are considering signing our student-athletes, the first three questions — in this order — they always ask are:

1] What is their GPA? (Grade Point Average)

2] Are they graduating on time?

3] Are they a good person?

Bottom line is, no matter how talented you might be, you can't move to the next level without good grades. The sooner you buy into that fact, the better your life will be.

So, yes, you may only be about thirteen years old, but what you do now is going to impact your future. This is all easier said than done; that is why visual (your actions) is always more important than audio (what you say) when determining who and what you will become.

Don't rule out a technical degree in your future. For whatever reason, a liberal arts education may not be for you. There is definitely no shame in a vocational career. There are a lot of adults out there making better money off of technical degrees as opposed to those with liberal arts degrees. I have spent my entire career as a teacher and coach. I received a liberal arts Associate of Arts degree, a Bachelor of Science degree in Education (major: Social Studies with a minor in Psychology and a coaching certification), and a Master of Science degree in Sports Management. I have enjoyed every minute of my career and make a good living with what I do. It required about seven years of post-high school education. Over the years I have met plumbers, carpenters, truck drivers, electricians, and computer technologists who are all making better money than I make and most of them have two-year technical degrees. On the other hand, I know doctors, lawyers, and dentists who make a lot more money and needed a minimum of eight years of college to get to where they are.

The key is to find something you are passionate about and really enjoy doing. It probably won't happen when you are thirteen, but when it does, lock-in and go for it. Along the way, every class, activity, club, organization, and part-time job you decide to take part in will help build your future and who you are.

Also start taking a close look at who you hang out with (friends, family, classmates, teammates, etc.).

Two schools of thought:

1] <u>All the people in your life can be divided into three categories.</u>

    A. ADDERS: People who make you better. They move you forward and enhance your life.

    B. MULTIPLIERS: Very special people. If you have one in your life, don't let them go. These people push you to places you never imagined for yourself. They lift you up to help you see a part of yourself that you may have never known existed. They will help you reach out to things you thought were beyond your grasp.

    C. SUBTRACTORS: They eat at you. They are a negative influence in your life. They hold you back and keep you from experiencing new people, places, activities, and interests. They put you down and keep you from moving forward. They cut into your self-esteem and make you feel bad. They are capable of talking you into unhealthy, unsafe, or unlawful activities. They monopolize your time for themselves.

    You must be leery of subtractors; they are deceptive. They can be what appears to be the cool kid; they might be your best friend or a boyfriend or girlfriend. For example, you want to join the choir but your best friend thinks it is stupid, so they talk you out of it because they want to spend more time with you.

    Simple formula for success: keep the adders and multipliers in your life and eliminate the subtractors.

2] <u>You are the average of your five closest friends.</u>

    Choose your friends wisely. It has been proven that we basically become who we spend most of our time with. If you want to get good grades, hanging out with people who don't study or do their homework is not a good idea. If you want to be healthy, hanging out with people who smoke or do drugs, again, is not a good idea.

    Remember I said you are the average of your five closest friends. You are your own person, but you are like the company you keep. People associate you with your friends, especially if they don't know you very well. Don't try to decide if this is right or wrong, but please understand it is true.

    After my college graduation, my mom asked me why I didn't graduate with honors. I told her because I wouldn't have been able to hang out with all my friends. We were all college graduates; one of my friends had a 4.0 grade point average, a couple squeaked by with 2.0+, and I came in around a 3.4.

# Mike Turnbull

When I talk to my student-athletes, I talk about staying above the crap. You will have ups and downs. You will meet good people and bad people. You will always have choices to make. Study/ Don't study; Go to class/ Don't go to class; Drink/Don't drink; Smoke/Don't smoke; Party/Don't party; Do drugs/ Don't do drugs; Have sex/Don't have sex; etc. You will make good and bad choices; we all do, no matter what age. Every decision we make has an impact on our lives and on the lives of others, and you have to hold yourself accountable for both good and bad decisions.

You have to keep asking yourself, "Who am I, what do I want to do with my life, and how do I want others to perceive me?" When you have the answers, ask yourself if your decisions, words, how you live your life, and your actions match up to your answers.

None of this is easy. Don't be afraid to seek counsel and guidance in others. I can't think of one person, myself included, other than Jesus Christ who wasn't or isn't flawed. Right now, picking your friends isn't easy. They could be a neighbor, somebody you have known for years. As you move on and start to find your niche in life, you start to get more selective and surround yourself with people who have similar interests and desires.

You don't have to take my word for this. You don't know me. Ask your parents, older relatives, a teacher, or a coach what they think. I'm saying most of my closest friends at this point in my life are people I met in college or during my career. Very few of my friends are someone I knew in elementary, middle, or high school.

I just thought I would throw this into the mix, because I can't find a better place to put it into the book. The following was written by Beverly Heirich. I do not know when it was written, and I do not know when I acquired it. I kept a copy several years ago and occasionally share it with my players. It is called "The Easy and the Hard." She starts by saying, "We all have the same question: Why is life so tough? Well, there's an answer to that . . ." Here are some excerpts:

*Bad is easy. Good is hard.*
*Losing is easy. Winning is hard.*
*Talking is easy. Listening is hard.*
*Watching TV is easy. Reading is hard.*
*Giving advice is easy. Taking advice is hard.*
*Flab is easy. Muscle is hard.*
*Stop is easy. Go is hard.*
*Dirty is easy. Clean is hard.*
*Take is easy. Give is hard.*
*Dream is easy. Think is hard.*

*Lying is easy. Truth is hard.*
*Sleeping is easy. Waking is hard.*
*Talking about God is easy. Praying to God is hard.*
*Watching basketball is easy. Playing basketball is hard.*
*Holding a grudge is easy. Forgiving is hard.*
*Telling a secret is easy. Keeping a secret is hard.*
*Play is easy. Work is hard.*
*Falling is easy. Getting up is hard.*
*Spending is easy. Saving is hard.*
*Eating is easy. Dieting is hard.*
*Doubt is easy. Faith is hard.*
*Laughter is easy. Tears are hard.*
*Criticizing is easy. Taking criticism is hard.*
*Letting go is easy. Hanging on is hard.*
*Secret sin is easy. Confession is hard.*
*Pride is easy. Humility is hard.*
*Excusing oneself is easy. Excusing others is hard.*
*Borrowing is easy. Paying back is hard.*
*Sex is easy. Love is hard.*
*Argument is easy. Negotiation is hard.*
*Naughty is easy. Nice is hard.*
*Going along is easy. Walking alone is hard.*
*Dumb is easy. Smart is hard.*
*Cowardice is easy. Bravery is hard.*
*Messy is easy. Neat is hard.*
*Poor is easy. Rich is hard.*
*War is easy. Peace is hard.*
*Sarcasm is easy. Sincerity is hard.*
*An F is easy. An A is hard.*
*Growing weeds is easy. Growing flowers is hard.*
*Reaction is easy. Action is hard.*
*Can't do is easy. Can do is hard.*
*Feasting is easy. Fasting is hard.*
*Following is easy. Leading is hard.*
*Having friends is easy. Being a friend is hard.*
*Dying is easy. Living is hard.*

Beverly Heirich closed out this list by writing: "If you ask why all this is so, why life is so hard, I'll tell you. 'It just is. Nothing in life that is good and worthwhile comes without effort.' We are all born with a nature that is drawn to the easy rather than the hard. Children don't need to be taught to be naughty; we are all born knowing how ... What's hard is learning to be good. Knowing this about one self and others softens the heart and builds iron into the will, keeps us going when all around is crumbling, when friends forsake, when the heart breaks, and the courage and confidence shatter.

"Knowing such experiences are part of the deal gives us opportunities to do hard things. Constant challenges make our journey exhilarating, wonderfully fulfilling, never, never boring. As the Arabs say, 'All Sunshine Makes a Desert.'

"Here's a small secret that most sad and lonely people never learn: Deep down inside we are all asking the same question. No matter who you are, life is hard, and we all ask why it should be so.

"But there is comfort in knowing we're not alone. So maybe your child—or the person sitting over there—needs to hear from you right this minute that sometimes you question, too, but the One who knows us best and loves us most promises that for those who choose the hard way, 'the dawn gives way to morning splendor while the evil grope and stumble in the dark.'"

Beverly closes with: "Easy is its own reward. Hard is much finer."

When I send out pre-season information packets to my student-athletes, I always include this list, titled, "What I won't do for my friends." By Mychal Wynn. I had planned to include it in the book but was unable to secure the permission to do so. I hate to do this to you but I am giving you a homework assignment. Please take the time to search: "What I won't do for my friends" by Mychal Wynn. Take the time to ingest and ponder what you read and share it with some friends. I am hoping you will find this exercise painless and well worth your time.

In case you have forgotten, this chapter was titled "Moving Forward." You may have picked up on the emphasis on friends and a support network. Whether intentionally or not, that is what it kept coming back to. Like all other advice, it is easier to give than to receive and, yes, as always easier said than done. To move forward and upward, you do need to choose your friends wisely; you will be the product of the people you choose to surround yourself with.

*Rise up!*
(Photo by Chris Brignola from Unsplash)

*Your time will come!*
(Photo by Skitter photo from Unsplash)

# Mike Turnbull

*Find your passion . . .*
(Photo by Joao Silas from Stock Snap)

*Stay in the race!*
(Photo by Nathan Shively from Unsplash)

*We can't all be number one!*
(Photo by Don Monroe)

# CHAPTER FIVE
## Don't Take My Word for It

I'm serious; if you are still reading this book, I'm happy, but please don't take what I have said up to this point as gospel. I'm just an average guy who has spent a career in the education system just sharing my experiences and thoughts.

When seeking advice, gather it from many sources, dissect it, mull it over, and decide for yourself what pertains to you and what you can use. I don't care if you get your information from books, newspapers, magazines, the internet, radio, television, social networking, or other people; process the information in your own head and heart, decide what you think, and act on it.

I have noticed with my own children and student-athletes that they have often accused me of doing some of the same things when I was young that they are doing now. You may have done that to your parents also, and at times you may feel they have forgotten what it feels like to be young. I want you to know that is far from the truth. Most of us adults cherish memories of our youth and they are etched in our minds. We remember the good and the bad things we did. We don't always openly share, but we remember.

Think about how sometimes your parents talk you into participating in an activity because they know how much they enjoyed it—or maybe it is something they didn't have the opportunity to do when they were young (camping, fishing, piano lessons, acting, singing, playing a sport, etc.). We are also quick to reprimand you when you do something that we don't approve of: smoking, skipping school, bullying, partying, breaking curfews, hanging out with questionable people, drinking, smoking pot, etc. Maybe it is because, yes, maybe we did the same things, but we don't want to see our mistakes duplicated by you. Most parents struggle with just letting you figure it out on your own. I thought there were some tough hurdles to get over growing up, but I will tell you I really don't know what is tougher than being a parent and trying to figure out the best way to go about it. Sometimes you have to cut your parents a little slack, because sometimes they are operating on a whim and a prayer. Just be thankful if you have parents who are there for you and are trying to do the best they can with the mom and dad thing. If you are without caring parents find a mentor, someone older to guide you. We all need a mentor. I am 56 years old and I still have several people in my life who I turn to for guidance.

Someone, much smarter than me, once said, "If we don't learn from our past we are doomed to repeat it." Okay; I wasn't sure if I had this right, so I Googled it. The quote is, "Those who cannot remember the past are condemned to repeat it." -George Santayana

I also came across another similar quote: "Those who don't know their history are doomed to repeat it. You have to expose who you are so that you can determine what you need to become." -Cynthia A. Patterson

As I said, someone much smarter than myself.

When you are having one of those days when you feel that life is tough, or being a kid is tough, and you want to lash out at your elders, take a moment and breathe. I want you to know that parenting, teaching, coaching or policing isn't easy, either. This isn't about keeping score; sometimes we just need to slow down and really listen to what each of us has to say. Adults need to spend a little more time just listening to kids, and kids need to give adults the same benefit. As adults, what we have to say or what we do is based in years of experience as kids and adults, and those of us with our priorities straight are just trying to help you figure life out. That all said, at some point it is up to you. It is called a life because you live it. You don't read about it or watch it, you live it!

I have vivid memories of teaching both my children to ride a bike. It started by them watching older kids ride bikes. Then I would have them watch me ride as I explained it to them. First they had tricycles, then two wheelers with training wheels. Next the training wheels came off and I would walk behind them, holding the seat so they wouldn't fall. Finally, one day I had to let go and see if they could handle it on their own. Not an easy thing to do, knowing they would most likely crash. All I could hope for was they would be okay and would want to get up and try it again. For me it was the letting go that was the hard part; for them it was finding out that a few scrapes and bruises could be overcome and riding that bike was fun and expanded their horizons. As they have grown older, there have been other times where it has come time to let go: the first time with a babysitter, first day of school, first school dance, first dates, driving a car, going away to college, starting their careers, and the toughest one: watching my daughter get married. Each time you just have to step back, you hope and pray you have taught them well and they have developed their own sense of will and direction. These are all just steps along the way when you are out there, living life.

As a parent, I did notice that when my children were young I was very smart. When they were teenagers, my wife and I were the dumbest people on the planet and did not understand anything about them, according to them. My children are grown now and starting families of their own. It seems my wife and I have regained our intelligence and wisdom, because they often seek our guidance in life matters. When I think about my own situation, I feel deep respect for my own parents and I really don't remember them being dumb or out of touch. I'm sure they probably were when I was a teenager, but I can't remember that very well. Funny how that works.

Just remember, you get bombarded with information every day. It comes at you in all forms; just take your time and sort it out. You have to decide for yourself: DELETE or SAVE?

*SAVE or DELETE?*
(Photo by freestock.org from Stock Snap)

*Never too old to believe!*

# Mike Turnbull

*Is the world ready for the next super hero?*
(Photo by Lexie Baack)

*Be thankful for Google and other search engines, this is how everyone used to do research!*
(Photo from Stocksnap/Snappa Photo by Redd Angelo)

# CHAPTER SIX
## High School & Beyond

Get ready for a great ride! You are about to enter into the most exciting, challenging, and fun part of your life. These will be the last years where you live life for yourself and have self-development as your primary focus. After post-secondary schooling, life becomes mostly about your spouse, family, and your job. Time for just you is few and far between.

Remember, if you want your life to be as fluid and easy as possible, keep the following in order:

*1] Graduate from high school.*
*2] Graduate from college/vocational school.*
*3] Get a job; start your career.*
*4] Get married. (Your call.)*
*5] Have children. (Again, your call.)*

Life is never an easy road as it is, but get any of these events out of order, or don't complete 1, 2, or 3, and life will be a whole lot more difficult.

Odds are you are entering the high school environment in ninth grade. Expect a somewhat rocky start; you are once again at the bottom of the pecking order—you have three grades above you. The next thing is, your grade now has a name: you are a freshman. Your sophomore, junior, and senior years will follow. Quick freshman joke: If you take two freshmen up in a helicopter 1,500 feet in the air and they both jump out at the same time, which one will hit the ground first? Answer: Who cares? They are just freshmen.

The first few days can be stressful; you'll get through it. There are new schedules, new buildings, new rules, locker combinations, new teachers, new coaches, etc. Take your time; you'll figure it all out. Don't try to go it alone. A lot of the most successful people are those who give of themselves and help others through the journey of life. There are a lot of people out there willing to help you; just ask. If you have some things figured out, offer to help classmates who don't.

One of the best things you can start doing for yourself right now is to begin working on getting a grip on time management. You are going to be really busy, and there will be a lot of demands put on your time. Just to name a few things: classes, activities, jobs, family, friends, homework, etc. You are going to have a great time, but you need to figure out how to balance your time and your life.

Don't take time for granted; it has a tendency to get away from you if you don't take the time to monitor it.

*Somebody has to steer.*
(Photo by Matthew Clark from Unsplash)

*Don't be in a rush
to grow up.*
(Photo by Lexie Baack)

*Celebrate the successes!*
(Photo by Don Monroe)

# TIME MANAGEMENT
## TIPS

1] Set your priorities and stick to them. Rank the five most important things in your life and evaluate whether you spend your time accordingly.

2] Schedule your days/weeks. Use some form of a planner.

3] Learn to say no! It is okay to say no to some people when you really don't have time to help them or join in some activity they are doing. You need to protect your time whenever you can.

4] At some point in the day, disconnect. Shut your phone off and get off the computer and turn off the television. Although they are an important part, and some might say a vital part, of our life, they also waste a lot of our time. You might also be surprised how relaxing a little quiet time can be.

5] Sleep! Your body and your mind need it. Tomorrow is always a lot longer and less productive if you don't sleep tonight.

6] Complete one task at a time. Multi-tasking is overrated. If I asked one student what they did yesterday and they said, "I started my homework, I started my voice lessons, I cut some of the grass in the yard, and I read a few pages in a book," I might ask another student the same question and they say, "I finished my homework, raked the yard, and cleared my text messages." Who would you say had a more productive day?

7] Learn to delegate. Personally, I have never mastered this one myself, but I recognize the value of it. You have to realize you can't do everything yourself; sometimes you need to request the help of others or have to ask them to complete a task for you to save time to do something else.

8] Nobody can ever have time management completely figured out. We should all stay open to new ideas that can help us with this skill. Incorporate what works for you and makes your life more manageable. Studies show that people who have successful careers and relationships tend to be people who manage their time well.

# CHAPTER SEVEN
## All the Best to You

I hope you find something in this book that helps you out. I wish you all the best in your middle school and high school years and beyond.

Keep your eye on the prize! The first prize is completing middle school and moving on to high school. The next prize is that high school diploma, which will open doors to anything you decide to do later.

Whatever you decide to do, work like you mean it, practice like you mean it, love like you mean it, and play like you mean it!

Stay true to yourself, your goals, your morals, and your beliefs! You are what makes you special. When it comes right down to it, a lot of people will have input, but you create you. Right now there is a you, but how exciting is it to think about the you that you will become!

You will meet a lot of new people and nurture new friends. No matter who comes in and out of your life, stay true to yourself and true to the people you can honestly say are your friends.

When I taught in secondary schools, I use to handout Mychal Wynn's "What I won't do for my friends." I gave it to all my students 7th–12th grades during the first week of school. I realize I mentioned Wynn's work on page 22, but if you haven't taken the time to look it up yet, now is the time. I realize what a big role your friends play in your life and I just want to drive this concept home. If more students bought into this concept there might be a lot less bullying taking place.

I know some of you might not take the time to look up "What I won't do for my friends" by Mychal Wynn, so here is one quote: "I won't disrespect, laugh at, or ridicule others for my friends."

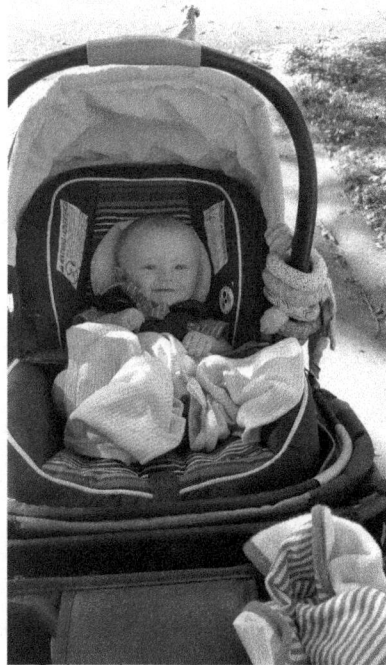

*It is going to be a great ride!*
(Photo by Lexie Baack)

33

*Take the backroads every once in a while and see the sites.*

*There is strength in numbers.*
(Photo by Don Monroe)

*There is wisdom in age and curiosity in youth; listen to each other.*

*Cherish your family.*
(Photo by Mike Loe)

# WHAT I WOULD NOT DO FOR MY FRIENDS

I realize that you have not all been dealt the same hand in life. You live in different places, go to different schools, and you have different household arrangements and different economic situations. That does not give you an excuse to fail or entitle you to succeed. You'll eventually realize that you have to work at everything worthwhile in your life.

We all have role models (good and bad) in our lives. Follow those who are successful and sincerely loved and respected for what they do and who they are. Keep your eye out for these people; they could be in your family, neighborhood, or school. They are out there; follow them and then take the lead!

Today is a great day to have a great day!

# WEBSITES YOU MIGHT WANT TO CHECK OUT

## Anti–Bullying
stopbullying.gov
www.pacerkidsagainstbullying.org
NoBullying.com

## Empowerment for Boys & Girls
www.girlsempowermentcenter.com
www.respestgirlsempowermentgroup.com/index.html
www.girlsinc.org
kidsempowerment.com
nexgenfoundation.blogspot.com
teens.drugabuse.gov
www.nutrition.gov/life-stages/adolescents/tweens-teens-and-teens

## Studying
www.how-to-study.com
www.studygs.net.attmot4.html

## Choosing a Career
www.iseek.org/parents/parentscareers.html
kids.usa.gov
www.myfuture.com
www.nationalscholastic.org/ncaa_clearing_house

## Inspiration
www.familyfriendpoems.com
www.goodreads.com/list/show/31320.most_inspirational_teen_books

# QUOTES TO CONTEMPLATE

"Right is right, even if everyone else is against it, and wrong is wrong, even if everyone is for it."
-William Penn

"You must be the change you want to see in the world."
-Ghandi

"All our dreams can come true, if we have the courage to pursue them."
-Walt Disney

"Talent is cheaper than table salt. What separates the talented individual from the successful one is a lot of hard work."
-Stephen King

"We never really grow up, we only learn how to act in public."
-Bryan White

"So many people try to grow up too fast, and it's not fun! You should stay a kid as long as possible."
-Vanessa Hudgens

"To an adolescent, there is nothing in the world more embarrassing than a parent."
-Dave Berry

"Youth comes but once in a lifetime."
-Henry Wadsworth Longfellow

"Good habits formed at youth make all the difference."
-Aristotle

"When I was growing up, my parents told me, finish your dinner. People in China and India are starving. I tell my daughters, finish your homework. People in China and India are starving for your job."
-Thomas Friedman

## Mike Turnbull

"A babysitter is a teenager acting like an adult while the adults are out acting like teenagers."
-Author Unknown

"Attitude is a little thing that makes a big difference."
-Winston Churchill

"Whatever you are, be a good one."
-Abraham Lincoln

"Music isn't for the eyes, it's for the ears."
-Adele

"Smile and let everyone know that today, you're a lot stronger than you were yesterday."
-Drake

"Don't spend all of your time trying to be like someone else because you can never be them and they can never be you."
-Raven Symone

"Normal is nothing more than a cycle on a washer machine."
-Whoopi Goldberg

"You don't need to look like everybody else. Love who you are."
-Lea Michele

"Make the right decision even when nobody's looking, and you will always turn out okay."
-Oprah Winfrey

"No matter what happens in life, be good to people. Being good to people is a wonderful legacy to leave behind."
-Taylor Swift

"No one will take care of you if you don't take care of yourself."
-Alicia Keys

"You can have the smallest role in the smallest production and still have a big impact."
-Neil Patrick Harris

"If there is any message in my work, it is ultimately okay to be different, that it is good to be different, that we should question ourselves before we pass judgement on someone who looks different, behaves different, is a different color."
-Johnny Depp

"If you are lucky enough to be different, don't ever change."
-Taylor Swift

"Beauty isn't judged by the size of your jeans."
-Jack Barakat

"If you tell the truth, you don't have to remember anything."
-Mark Twain

"For every dark night, there is a brighter day."
-Tupac Shakur

"I love myself and if you could say the same you wouldn't be sitting on your computer trying to hurt others."
-Miley Cyrus

"Be yourself; everyone else is already taken."
-Oscar Wilde

"No one can make you feel inferior without your consent."
-Eleanor Roosevelt

"Darkness cannot drive out darkness: only light can do that. Hate cannot drive out hate: only love can do that."
-Martin Luther King Jr.

"Fairy tales are more than true, not because they tell us that dragons exist, but because they tell us that dragons can be beat."
-G.K. Chesterton

"Not all of us can do great things. But we can do small things with great love."
-Mother Teresa

## Mike Turnbull

"When one door of happiness closes, another opens; but often we look so long at the closed door that we do not see the one which has opened for us."
-Helen Keller

"Failure is a great teacher and if you are open to it, every mistake has a lesson to offer."
-Oprah Winfrey

"Things work out best for those who make the best of how things work out."
-John Wooden

"You miss 100% of the shots you never take."
-Michael Jordan

"Absorb what is useful, Discard what is not, Add what is uniquely your own."
-Bruce Lee

"When the power of love overcomes the love of power, the world will know peace."
-Jimmy Hendrix

"The future belongs to those who prepare for it today."
-Malcolm X

# ABOUT THE AUTHOR

(Photo by Mike Flaten)

I am 56 years old, and my wife Pam and I have lived in Hibbing, MN, for the past nineteen years. I coach and teach at Hibbing Community College, and Pam runs the Mitchell-Tappan House Bed & Breakfast in Hibbing. Pam and I own and live in the B&B, but she is the Innkeeper and I claim to be the Groundskeeper; either way, she is the boss and does a great job.

Pam and I have been married for thirty-four years and have two grown children. Lexie lives and works in Nebraska with her husband, Jeff, and our grandson, Beckett. Lexie is a high school volleyball coach and choir accompanist. Jeff is a farmer, and Beckett is not gainfully employed (he is 5 months old). Our son, Blaine, lives in Minneapolis, MN, and works as a counselor at a juvenile detention center. He and his fiancé, Alex, will be married this summer.

I grew up the son of Jack and Patricia Turnbull and have three younger sisters, Terri, Lisa, and Stacie. My dad was a career Navy man, so we moved all over the country. He retired from the Navy in 1975, and we moved to Ely, MN, where I started my junior year of high school.

I received my A.A. degree from Vermilion Community College in Ely, MN, in 1979. I received my Bachelor's degree from Bemidji

State University in Bemidji, MN, in 1981 and my Master's degree from the United States Sports Academy in Daphne, AL, in 1990.

I have taught and coached for the past 35 years all over Minnesota; twelve years in secondary schools and twenty-three years at the college level. I have cherished every minute of my career.

In my 56 years on this earth, enough to qualify as an AARP member and senior discounts at most restaurants, I can't pretend to have figured everything out, but I do think I have a somewhat unique story to tell, and I hope it strikes a chord with those of you who read it. I have had these thoughts for as long as I can remember, and I've managed to write a few of them down for you to ponder and consider.

Now, I have written my fourth book and I am very excited to have the opportunity to share it with you. It is my first attempt at writing a book for young readers. I hope you enjoy reading it as much as I have enjoyed writing it. It is an extremely humbling and rewarding experience to put your thoughts to writing and share them with the public.

I feel blessed that Rivershore Books has agreed to publish my fourth book, and I look forward to future projects with them.

I have always taken pride in being referred to as "Coach," second to my favorite titles of "Husband," "Dad," and most recently "Grandpa Mike." I never dreamed I would see "Author" in front of my name.

"A GUIDE TO MIDDLE SCHOOL & BEYOND"
Mike Turnbull, November 17, 2015

# Coach Mike Turnbull's
# COACHING PHILOSOPHY

My coaching philosophy is a simple one. I treat my student-athletes as people first, students second, and athletes third. In all my thoughts, words, and actions, I attempt to teach the young adults that I coach to be good people first, responsible and successful students second. The last point of focus is the level of performance as athletes.

In being concerned with my student-athletes socially and academically as well as athletically, my commitment goes well beyond the court, field, and immediate years I spend coaching them. I realize they are adults, but I also feel that any positive guidance I can lend them is time and energy well spent.

Over the years, I have experienced many successes and defeats with my players. I have always felt proud of the positive accomplishments that we have experienced in the realm of athletics. I can honestly say, my proudest moments have come when I've seen them graduate or heard of their successful careers or that they have turned out to be solid citizens.

I feel winning is important, but I also feel that the truly meaningful lessons in athletics come from learning to do the everyday physical, mental, and emotional work and preparation that is necessary to position oneself for the opportunity to win. These are the lessons that are taken from participation in athletics that help us be successful people, students, employees, and community and family members. These lessons, if learned honestly, will help us for a lifetime.

In conclusion, as I coach I am also a role model, and it is not only important to tell student-athletes that this is my philosophy, but also to show them in my actions: how I treat people and how I live out my daily life. My family is the most important aspect of my life, and I have always treated my teams as an extension of my family.

# BOOKS BY
# MIKE TURNBULL

*All the books are published by Rivershore Books & available in E-book & printed versions.

RANDOM THOUGHTS OF A STUPID MAN

MORE RANDOM THOUGHTS OF A STUPID MAN

STILL A STUPID MAN

A GUIDE TO MIDDLE SCHOOL & BEYOND

Available in e-books and printed versions.

<u>Available at:</u>

www.rivershorebooks.com
www.amazon.com
www.barnesandnoble.com
www.nookpress.com
www.smashwords.com
Piragasis' Northwoods Store: Ely, MN
Mitchell-Tappan House Bed and Breakfast: Hibbing, MN

# RIVERSHORE BOOKS

www.rivershorebooks.com
info@rivershorebooks.com
www.facebook.com/rivershore.books
www.twitter.com/rivershorebooks
blog.rivershorebooks.com
forum.rivershorebooks.com

www.ingramcontent.com/pod-product-compliance
Lightning Source LLC
Chambersburg PA
CBHW071433040426
42445CB00012BA/1354